Published by
FORMING LIVES

MY BEST ME - Textbook 6

Editor-In-Chief
Josien Knigge

Authors
Melanie Martinez
Anne Marie Wahls
Elizabeth Palmer Solon
Josien Knigge

Editors
Anne Marie Wahls
Elizabeth Palmer Solon

Revision and Correction
Kyle Duncan
Suzanne Duncan
Josien Knigge

Cover Design
Ziza Zoe Malloy

ISBN-13: 978-1-951061-00-5

Forming Lives Inc.
PO Box 722255
Norman, OK 73070
United States
Tel: (405) 561-1717
Email: info@forminglives.com
www.forminglives.com

4.0.6.usa

Seven Life Principles

"My Best Me" is a guide to help you discover who you are and who you are becoming... your true identity. This program is founded on seven life principles that give you the tools to develop your social and emotional skills (also known as EQ, or emotional intelligence).

LOVE
To give

The conscious decision to care for others

CREATION
To speak

The desire to transform thoughts into reality

PURPOSE
To direct

The ability to understand your role within your family and community

WORK
To serve

The desire to provide for others

PRODUCTIVITY
To be fruitful

The passion to use your talents to create results

LEADERSHIP
To manage

The motivation to manage natural and human resources

FAMILY
To accept

The compassion to accept and harmonize with someone who is different than you

Five Key Concepts

In the text you will find five units that form the building blocks of a society, which will be used to train students. They will facilitate the use of this book.

IDENTITY
Discover who I am

My role
My personality
My character

HEALTH
Discover how to maintain order

Physical
Mental
Emotional

COMMUNITY
Discover how to interact with others

Family
People like me
People different from me
Strangers

ENVIRONMENT
Discover why and how to
manage nature

Natural resources
Plant life
Animal life

ECONOMICS
Discover the difference between
wealth, value, and true success

Needs versus wants
Financial balance
Resource management

Understanding the Icons

 READ

A story, a poem, a saying or a script that adds to the subject

 UNDERSTAND

To gain knowledge, insight, and understanding through information

 OBSERVE

To look, see, find, watch, and discover more

 CREATE

To paint, color or make in a personal way

 GAME

Engage in an experience and discovery together

 WRITE

To write, mark, or sketch personal ideas or discoveries

 CONCLUSION

A closing statement on the lesson subject with a final thought

 APPLY

To bring into action, put to use, and demonstrate understanding

 SHARE

A contribution, present or suprise to share with others

 ACTIVITY

A task that involves direct experience and action

 COMMENT

Discuss, consider, or examine certain subjects

 REFLECT

Think, ponder, meditate or wonder about important issues

 MUSIC

To learn, write, sing or listen to a song, enjoy a harmony of sounds

 VIDEO

Watch a clip or film section and analyze the information

CONTENTS

Identity

Health

Community

Environment

Economics

Introduction

Have you ever had an adult ask you, "What do you want to do when you grow up?" It's a great question, but sometimes hard to answer. After all, you have a lot of time to figure out your future career! "My Best Me" is not so much about helping you discover what kind of job you want to do when you grow up, but more about helping you decide what kind of person you want to be.

In this book, we will explore what we call the "building blocks" or foundations of becoming a well-rounded person who engages with others and their world in a healthy, productive way. By discovering your gifts and talents, and learning how to use them to successfully navigate the challenges of life, you will become the person you were destined to be.

We hope you enjoy this course and gain a greater understanding of the unique strengths and talents that make you, you!

IDENTITY

Discover who you are, what personality you were born with, how to develop your character, and key roles in your life.

Having a healthy sense of your own identity gives you authority and confidence.

It allows you to be a person of influence who is not easily swayed by the circumstances or pressures of life.

It releases you to use your unique leadership qualities to impact the world with who you are.

Why Am I the Way I Am?

 Goal — To discover and understand that each of us is unique and different for a specific reason

Read

Sarah was a cheerful and energetic girl; she always had great ideas and everyone wanted to spend time with her. She was the oldest of three sisters and loved by her parents. However, as she grew older, she realized that she was a lot shorter than the other students. Even her younger sisters were taller than her. Every day she made a wish to grow a little more and be taller. Unfortunately, her wish never came true.

Later, she graduated from college and had to choose a career. Without hesitation she chose to be a preschool teacher because she loved children and connected with them very well. When she began to work with the little children, she realized her great advantage. She was closer to the children because of her height, and did not have to spend all day crouching and kneeling to help them at their level.

 Write: Complete the table with your characteristics in the following areas

Physical (e.g., tall, brown eyes)	Intellectual (e.g., good at math, studious)	Emotional (e.g., caring, dependable)

 Comment

In what ways are you different from your classmates?
In what ways are you similar to your classmates?

 Understand

People spend a lot of time trying to change themselves to fit in with a group. Imagine how life would be if we took more time to celebrate the differences between us and

appreciate each other's remarkable qualities. Our differences and individual character traits are the ingredients that make the world unique and interesting.

Because we are different, we are able to fulfill a great variety of roles in our communities. We have artists, bankers, teachers, musicians, business people, and other occupations. Each of these roles require individuals with specific qualities, abilities, talents, interests and characteristics. It is due to our individuality that a person can find a new path, invent something, or write a song. Each of us were made the way we are to fulfill our specific and special role. Like a puzzle, each personality fits together to create our community.

Unfortunately, we often categorize and label individuals whom we perceive to be different from us. It takes courage to be different, and strength to accept the differences of others. And sometimes, others will not understand our unique qualities in the same way that we don't understand theirs. Being willing to take risks and be different is like a fish swimming against the current. It is not always easy, but the outcome is worth it!

Activity: Circle your Characteristics

Athletic	Perfectionist	Trustworthy	Creative	Outgoing
Talkative	Caring	Optimistic	Happy	Introverted
Generous	Kind	Quiet	Shy	Artistic
Silly	Thoughtful	Temperamental	Grumpy	Brave
Messy	Compassionate	Organized	Respectful	Peacemaker

After circling your characteristics, get into groups of three and pass around your work. Have other students use a different colored pen or pencil to circle what they think your characteristics are. After they are done, compare.

Reflect

When you think about Sarah, are you reminded of your own flaws or "defects"? Could your "defect" actually have the hidden potential to be a strength (like Sarah's height)?

I am unique and have a special role within my community.

Ups and Downs

To learn that I am able to control my emotions

News of The Day · 8m
Vehicles Crash, Passengers and Driver Clash

At about 8:00 AM this morning, a car crashed head on into the side of a crowded bus on Main Street. Many passengers were hurt and shaken up. Two of the passengers stepped off of the bus and attacked the driver of the car, verbally as well as physically.

Read

Is there a difference between aggression, frustration, and anger? Explain.

_____

_____

Is there a difference between sadness, grief, and depression? Explain.

_____

_____

"Do not let the sun go down while you are still angry." Explain the meaning of this advice and share it with the class.

_____

_____

How could the passengers on the bus have controlled their anger more appropriately?

_____

_____

 Video

Take time to watch this clip.

 Understand

Scientists have classified human emotions in certain basic groups: happiness, acceptance, fear/dread, surprise, sadness, disgust, anger and anticipation (when we look forward to something). For example, behind the emotion of jealousy is fear, behind joy is acceptance.

flives.us/?i=96021

We take control of our lives and our circumstances when we control our emotions. It is important to recognize our emotions, own them, and avoid denying them. Recognizing our emotions does not mean that we should let them control us. Rather, we should

understand what causes the emotions and how they make us feel. In doing so, we will learn to manage them appropriately.

We decide how to react to the emotions we feel. Willpower is the extent of control that we have over our actions. For example, you often hear people say, "He made me mad." This is a false statement. The other person does not make you mad, you allow yourself to become angry. You have complete control over your own actions and reactions. When you discover this, you realize the extent of your influence on others. For example, your will to control your anger determines your actions. You can let it be a minor frustration, or a major blow up. Learning to manage your emotions is an ongoing process.

 Apply

Identify an emotion and how you react to it.

For example: I become angry when someone takes something that belongs to me. I react by yelling at the person. Instead, I can calmly ask the person to give it back.

I become _____

when _____.

I react by _____.

Instead, I can _____

_____

 Reflect

How do you feel about the emotions you sense others are experiencing?
How can you control your emotions so they don't negatively affect your family and friends?

I have a positive influence on myself and others when I control my emotions.

Vital Friendships

To learn how to be a good friend

Activity: Complete the Sentence

Friendship is _____

The qualities that I bring to a friendship are _____

I expect my friends to be _____

Write:

These are the qualities I look for in a friend

- _____
- _____
- _____
- _____

Self Evaluation - mark the answer that best describes the truth for you.

Attitude	Always	Rarely	Never
I make fun of my peers.			
I am respectful toward my peers.			
I bully my classmates.			
I stick up for my peers.			
I can relate to other students' feelings.			
I can be rude and mean toward my classmates.			
I understand my peers.			
I show my friends that I care about them.			
I encourage my peers to do positive things.			
I tell my friends when they do something I don't agree with.			

Understand

Having friends brings many benefits to our lives. A friend is a person who is sincere, honest, and loyal, who accepts us and does not judge us. We trust our friends to keep secrets, both big and small. A friend helps us to enhance our life by seeking new adventures and encouraging us to connect with others who will improve our life. A friend is someone who can confront us if they feel we are making bad choices. Friendships increase our own confidence and happiness level, and at the same time help us to find meaning and direction in our lives.

It is important to analyze what kind of friend we are since we know what a vital role friends play. Do we deserve the title FRIEND? Are we individuals who look after the welfare of others when someone is in need? Can others trust us? When someone does something negative or dangerous, do we confront him or her? These questions help us evaluate how to be a better friend ... someone in life that makes you laugh a little louder, smile a little bigger, and live just a little bit better.

Activity

- A classmate is elected to coach the game and untie the "human knot."
- The others create a "human knot" making a circle, but instead of grabbing the hands of those next to them, the students grab one hand of two different classmates across or further away from them.
- When all are holding hands, the classmate who is directing begins to undo the knot, giving instructions to all his/her friends of how to get untangled without letting go of the hands. Discover if this is possible.
- Take turns leading the game.
- What was your experience with untying the "human knot" of friendship?

Reflect

How can you improve your friendships and be a better friend?

I am a wonderful friend because I want to have friends.

My Values

To learn to hold true to my values and principles

Read

Hunter "Patch" Adams was born in Washington DC on December 29, 1943. His experience in a psychiatric hospital inspired him to study medicine in the late 60s. Patch was constantly criticized by his teachers because of his "excessive joy."

Adams was convinced that doctors were more concerned with patients' illnesses instead of the patients themselves. By then he had a vision to help the patient as a whole to live a more fulfilled life. He believed that people were healthy if they were living a happy life. For instance, people who are dying of cancer or are very sick can potentially improve their condition or at least be happier. It is possible, as long as they have a positive outlook and attitude toward life.

flives.us/?i=96041

After graduating from medical school in 1974, Adams founded the Gesundheit! Institute, a unique hospital that functioned in a house in the plains of Virginia. He took in patients that had no way of paying, and treated them for free. He gave them hope and reassurance in their time of desperation. He longed to have a large, state-of-the art facility, but that would have to wait, as he did not have the resources.

Currently, Patch spends around two thirds of the year traveling the world, giving seminars and workshops to spread his life philosophy. He believes that the world has a deficit of hugs, and without love and acceptance the world will get worse.

Comment:
What makes Patch Adams special?
Write at least one of your personal values.

Understand

"Who am I?" This is an important question to ask yourself. We are the result of a fusion of a natural, mental, social and spiritual background. The first five years of our life are spent learning from those around us by observation. Most of the behaviors we learn in those first few years are retained (remembered) for the rest of our lives, and have great impact on how we behave. Of course, the DNA we inherit from our parents determines our biological characteristics. Our parents or guardians also teach us how to handle our emotions, react to our environment, and treat people. This forms the basis of our own "moral code." In other words, the set of values and beliefs that determine the decisions we make as we grow into adulthood.

As we grow up and mature, we start to show our potential and talents, which are often linked to our dreams and intertwined with our values. Only individuals who are willing to go against the flow, leave their comfort zone, and endure rejection will display their talents to the fullest and fulfill their dreams, like Patch Adams.

Activity: Autobiographical Essay

Write an essay about your life: tell your family's story, including what values are important to them; how do they connect to your own interests, talents and dreams?

Reflect

Ponder your list of values and talents. (Use page 24 for your personal notes.)
How can you use your talents (linked to your values) to help and serve others?

I will go against the flow and fulfill my dreams.

Lesson 5

My Talent Shines Through

Goal To be aware of my strengths and talents and use them toward a bright future

 Activity: Analysis of your abilities and interests

What day of the week (between Monday and Friday) is your favorite?

_____

What subjects do you have that day?

_____

Which of the above-mentioned subjects is your favorite? Why?

_____

Do you prefer to do activities that include physical action and being outside, or indoor activities that are more calm and quiet?

_____

What are four professions that interest you? Why?

_____

What skills do you have? In what areas are you skillful or capable?

_____

In what profession or job do you think you can best put your skills to work?

_____

_____

If money were not an obstacle, what would you do all day? Why?

_____

_____

💬 **Comment**
Looking at your answers, what conclusions can you make about a type of career you could have? Which of your skills will you need to develop for your future job?

16

Understand

Being original means we are unique—there is no one like us in all the Earth. This is great! We do not need to be like others, nor do what others do. We can be ourselves; originals, not copies. However, it takes courage to be who we are.

We are born with personal characteristics that make us unique. For example, some people are natural runners. From a very young age they are fast and graceful at running. Other skills, however, we discover and develop over time. What comes easily to one person, might take years of practice for another. This can be frustrating at times, but it is important to remember that we are all different and we all excel in distinct areas of life.

Each one of us is born with talents. It is up to us to develop those skills through determination, discipline, and training to use them in a productive way. By recognizing our own strengths, we can achieve the goals we set in life. To develop skills in specific areas at a young age means we can make a bigger impact in the future. Our talents can lead us to do great things, with both our own lives and in the lives of others.

Write

Though we are often taught to be modest, now is your chance to "toot your own horn." Write an essay honestly describing your strengths, talents, and skills. Explain where these skills will lead you in life, and what goals they will help you to accomplish. Imagine that you are "selling yourself" and informing the world of all the amazing things you will achieve. You are someone special, and don't be afraid to say it!

Reflect

How can you further develop the strengths, skills, and talents you already have?

I identify my creativity and skills and know what to do to reach my set goals.

Lesson 6

Finding Balance

Goal To learn to find balance in my life in order to have inner peace and confidence

 Game

Follow the directions your teacher gives you. After completing the game, answer the following questions with your group:

- What happens to the tower if one of the pieces is not balanced with the rest?
- How did you feel when it was your turn to remove a piece and then add a piece to the tower?
- Have you ever felt like that in your own life? Explain?
- When each of the four people work together, what happens?

 Understand

Now imagine the tower is an individual and each of the four members of the group represents the important aspects that help the tower, or that person, maintain balance in their life. Just like our group of four worked together to build the tower and at the same time kept it from falling down, each of us consists of four different aspects that are tied together and needed for our growth (see illustration below). It is important for us to learn how to maintain and nurture these aspects to keep our life and self balanced and not fall in pieces.

These four parts of our being are the inner self, our emotions (and social aspect), the mind, and the body. When we nurture and develop these four areas equally, we attain balance and experience inner peace and satisfaction This then helps us stay focused and have confidence in ourselves.

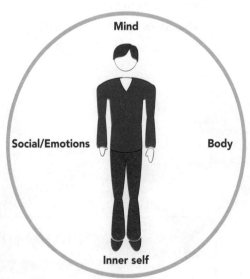

Unfortunately, due to the nature of life and its many challenges, we often find ourselves out of balance. Such imbalances can leave us feeling upset, dissatisfied, and insecure. What happens when we feel this way? What can we do to get ourselves back in balance and build our "tower" back up again?

Read: Let's look at each aspect of ourselves

Mind: This is the aspect with which we think, perceive, learn, remember, decide, imagine, desire, etc. It is where we store our memories and the things we learn. We can strengthen our mind with reading, reflecting, observing, repetition, brain challenges, structuring, information, and many other activities.

Body: This is the mechanical or physical part of our being; our organs, bones, nerves, blood vessels, lymphatic system, muscles, etc. We can strengthen it through a healthy diet, daily exercise/activity, hygiene and adequate rest.

Inner self: This is the moral aspect of our being, our conscience or intuition. Creativity is birthed in this aspect of our being. We can develop it by serving others (love), increasing in wisdom, living out our beliefs and convictions.

Emotional (social): This aspect has to do with how we relate, interact, and communicate with others and our environment. We can strengthen it through friendships, community activities, and an open and positive attitude toward those around us.

 Activity: Short Story (Written over 2 Days)

1. With a partner, write a rough draft of a short story that includes a main character who has an imbalance in their life, and reflects the aspect you were assigned by your teacher (i.e., inner self, emotional, mind, or body). Do not resolve the imbalance in the story; leave the ending open.
2. Exchange rough drafts with another group. After receiving peer edits, do a final draft and share.
3. Again exchange stories with another group, and imagine the character in the story you are reading is a friend. Based on what you have learned about the four aspects that keep us balanced, write a conclusion to the other group's story that includes a solution to help the character become balanced again.
4. Once you have finished, return the story to the classmates who started it.

Reflect

What are some ways that you can improve the balance in your own life?

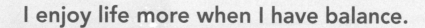

I enjoy life more when I have balance.

Trust

To discover who loves me and has my best interests at heart

Read

A bridge is a connection between two points across some kind of obstacle. It provides access to both sides, which allows an exchange of products, information, services and people that are key for communication and development.

Bridges are usually built better structurally if they are expected to support high traffic. The pillars that support bridges require specific calculations and engineering to know how and where to place them, so they don't collapse. Most bridges are large and imposing structures.

Activity

Form a circle, where each student faces the center. Stand close to the student next to you, and stretch your arms straight in front of you with palms open. One person stands in the middle of the circle with their arms crossed in front of their chest, eyes closed and legs straight and locked. This person either leans back or forward, the group members catch him/her, and carefully passes or pushes him/her to the next partner, always making sure the individual is in the center. Exchange places until the entire group has passed through the center of the circle.

 Comment

Did you trust your classmates not to drop you? Why/why not?
After observing your classmates on how they treated the person in the middle, would you describe them as trustworthy? Why/why not?

 Understand

Each of us operates inside a family. Those living with us on a daily basis often know us best, and can give wise advice based on their knowledge and interest in us. The older generations can sympathize with our problems because they have already passed through this stage. Much like the bridge, older generations can serve as pillars of trust in our life as they help us connect our present and "cross over" to our future.

Teachers can also be like pillars in our life as they help us become successful, confident adults. The same is true with reliable friends who can be as close as family and love us the same. They have our best interests in mind and care enough to tell us the truth. Support from and connection with our family, friends, and teachers is vital.

If we are able to trust those who love us, it will allow us to be confident, knowing that we have that support.

Explain three situations when your parents or mentors have been pillars in your life. After, share details of each situation with a partner.

- _____
- _____
- _____

Reflect

Name at least one person in your life whom you can trust.
How have they earned your trust?
How can you be a trustworthy person for your friends and family?

There are people in my life who have earned my trust.

Lesson 8

Embracing Change

To learn that I can manage change and make it a positive experience

Understand

As we enter our teenage years, much change is coming our way. And changes can often bring feelings of uncertainty. Activities we used to enjoy may now be uncomfortable or make us feel awkward because of what our friends might think or say. We might at times feel clumsy, uncoordinated, and out of harmony with our surroundings which can create a sense of isolation. We may find that our emotions are positive and bright one moment, and the next second everything feels full of doom and gloom as nothing seems to be going right.

To grow and be successful, change is a necessary part of life. We decide how we approach and accept change, whether it will be exciting and exhilarating or stressful and draining. The more flexible we are in adapting to these new and different changes, the fewer struggles we will experience.

Think of a kayak: the more it fills up with water, the more bogged down it becomes, making it slow and more difficult to manage. If it remains dry, however, it easily glides through the changing currents and waves it encounters. In the same way, we can weigh down our life by taking the changes we experience too seriously. Or, we can try to manage the changes in our life by going with the flow and the changes we experience.

Game

You will play two games to experience what change does to you. The teacher will explain the rules.
1. Fold your arms
2. Change your look

Write

What does the word "stagnant" mean? _____

_____

What can happen if water is stagnant? _____

_____

What happens if air is stagnant? _____

What will happen to your life if it becomes stagnant?

Physically _____

Emotionally _____

Mentally _____

Observe

With a partner, find a quote or saying that reflects your current feelings toward change. You can use a quote already written by someone else (be sure to give them credit), or write one yourself. Then, express in your own words what you think this quote is trying to communicate.

For example: "When you are finished changing, you're finished" – Benjamin Franklin. Significance: The reason to live disappears if you stop changing.

_____

_____

Create

Find four images or pictures that you like (i.e., images from a magazine, printed from an online source, etc.). Cut or tear each of the prints into smaller pieces. Glue all the pieces of the four images on a sheet of cardstock paper in a new way. Your new art is just like you as you experience changes in your life. How you look or feel may change as you grow, but you are still you, just in a new way.

Once you are done, present your artwork to some of your classmates.

Reflect

What has been the greatest change that has happened in your life lately? How did you feel about that change?

Looking back at the change you experienced, did it help you in any manner?

I face change with excitement and expectation, because it allows me to grow and be innovative.

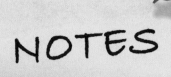

NOTES

Health

Discover how to grow and thrive physically, mentally, emotionally, and socially by keeping order and balance in your life.

Consistently maintaining your health will increase your energy level, protect you against disease, and improve your overall appearance and mental capacity.

Your health is an essential building block to you fulfilling your destiny and living a life of satisfaction, overflowing with happiness and strong self-worth.

My Beautiful Body

Goal To learn and train myself to think constructively and more positively about my appearance and body

Activity
Progressive muscle relaxation/Imagery - This activity will give you better control over your thoughts. Listen to your teacher as he/she guides you through the activities.

Read
Automatic thoughts are brief thoughts that spring up suddenly and quickly. We are often barely aware of these thoughts, but usually quite aware of the emotions that result from them. We tend to accept these automatic thoughts as true.

With some effort, we can learn to block these thoughts and change them into more constructive and positive ones. If a person is able to exchange unwanted thoughts for healthier ones, he/she will be much more likely to feel comfortable with their appearance and who they are. And even more, they will experience a rise in their confidence level.

Comment: Are the following statements true or false?
- Physically attractive people have it all.
- I wish I was better looking.
- The first thing people notice about me is what is wrong with my appearance.
- The media's message makes beauty standards impossible.
- If I could change_____I would be happier.
- My happiness depends on my appearance.
- My happiness depends on me accepting myself and fulfilling what I was created to do.

Understand

The media portrays people as perfect by photoshopping and filtering their photos and appearances. We grow up constantly looking at these "perfect" images and think we need to look a certain way in order to be happy. NO ONE, not even the models, is perfect. Everyone has perceived faults and things they would like to change about themselves!

How can we learn to be comfortable (and even happy) with who we are, and love ourselves, despite our perceived flaws? The first step is to identify the thoughts we think about ourselves. If we constantly feed ourselves negative messages about our body, comparing ourselves with others, we will be stuck in a destructive pattern of how we see ourselves. If we learn to embrace our perceived flaws, understand they make us the unique person we are, and that those "flaws" can even add to our appearance and impact, we will be much more confident and happy.

Apply

If you decide you want to change the way you think about yourself and experience greater confidence, here is a tip. Use the following methods to change negative automatic thoughts into positive ones.

- With eyes closed think of "a place of peace" that you love—a beach, mountain stream, or perhaps lounging with a pet in the sun—and take slow breaths as you "see" that calming place in your mind. Repeat this exercise when needed.
- Identify your negative thoughts and exchange them for positive ones. Close your eyes and imagine taking that negative thought and placing it on the returns counter at a local store, and then "exchanging" it for a positive one.
- Talk to a friend or family member who makes you feel good about yourself and your strengths.

Reflect

How are you going to maintain a positive attitude about your body, your appearance, and yourself?

By improving my thought process I will increase my confidence and energy.

My Amazing Brain

To understand that my intelligence and talents are not fixed, but change and grow over time

Video
Take time to watch this clip: flives.us/?i=96101

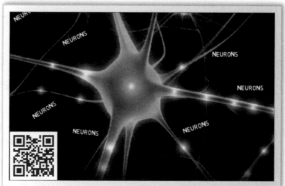

flives.us/?i=96101

Understand

Over 30 years ago, Dr. Carol Dweck of Stanford University began to study why some students are easily discouraged when they fail, while others are not as affected. She found through numerous studies about students' behavior that the brain is changeable and can get "stronger" (smarter), like a muscle. The key was how the students dealt with the letdowns they encountered. This is called grit—courage, determination, and toughness.

You "grow" your brain. You decide to take charge of how you learn.

For example, Thomas Edison's teachers said he was "too stupid to learn anything." He was fired from his first two jobs for being "non-productive." As an inventor, Edison made 1,000 unsuccessful attempts at inventing the light bulb. When a reporter asked, "How did it feel to fail 1,000 times?" Edison replied, "I didn't fail 1,000 times. The light bulb was an invention with 1,000 steps." Each step brought him closer to the final victorious result. https://www.uky.edu/~eushe2/Pajares/OnFailingG.html

Edison had a Growth Mindset. He kept challenging the curiosity within him, pressing through disappointments and letdowns. He didn't view himself as a failure, but used his grit to keep pressing through. We all fall down, but we choose whether or not to climb out of that pit.

We have the choice to see our mistakes as opportunities to get smarter and learn from them. Or, we can believe that we are failures and that we will never understand or conquer whatever is challenging for us.

Thomas Edison

 Activity

Identify something that you feel you are limited in or unsuccessful at. For example: "I am lousy in math, just like my parents."

I am_____

Now make a list of 3 things you can do that will help you have a Growth Mindset in your "weak" area above.

1. _____
2. _____
3. _____

Share the list with a partner. Over the next 21 days take note when anything improves after trying these 3 things. Come back after this "21 Day Challenge" and see what difference it made in your life, and in the life of your class partner.

Reflect

Why is having a Growth Mindset important for your future? How can having a Growth Mindset help you overcome an obstacle you are facing today?

✔ **When I apply myself, keep trying, and refuse to give up, I will grow and improve.**

My Plate, My Fate?

Goal — To learn how my nutritional habits influence all aspects of my life

✏️ **Write: Complete the following phrase and compare it with your classmates'.**

When I am hungry, the first thing I generally want to eat is: _____

My favorite beverage is: _____

My favorite restaurant is: _____

I usually eat _____ (#) vegetables and _____ (#) fruits in a day.

When I feel sad or discouraged I eat: _____

A few foods I dislike are: _____

Where I sit or walk when I eat is: _____

I eat _____ times a day.

Do I eat alone or do I eat with others? _____

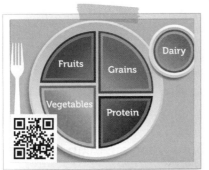

flives.us/?i=96091

💡 **Understand**

The image to the left, called *Myplate,* is a good reminder of what portion size we should eat of each food group at every meal. Teenagers grow and mature at a rapid rate, and gain approximately 20% of their size and 50% of their weight during this stage. It's critical to learn healthy eating habits at this age by focusing on variety, balance, amount, quality, timing, location, and nutritional value. As you do, you set the stage for a lifelong discipline and a healthier future.

The MyPlate program, one of many, emphasizes the importance of healthy eating and states that starting with small changes can eventually build into all-around healthier eating habits. One of the first important steps is that we choose foods and beverages with less saturated fat, sodium, and added sugars.

The *MyPlate.gov* website says, "Eating healthy is a journey shaped by many factors, including our stage of life, situations, preferences, access to food, culture, traditions, and the personal decisions we make over time. All your food and beverage choices count. MyPlate offers ideas and tips to help you create a healthier eating style that meets your individual needs and improves your health." Visit *Myplate.gov* to find healthy eating tips, meal/exercise trackers, and other important resources to help you live a healthy lifestyle (www.choosemyplate.com, 2016).

Read

The mind/body connection is the relationship between our physical and social/emotional self. We may notice that when we eat healthy foods and eat in communion (harmony) with others that our mood is better, we think more sharply, and we are less irritable. That is the mind/body connection. Have you ever sat around the table with family or friends, taking the time and attention to enjoy a wonderful meal together? Did you experience a joyful and satisfying moment when you did this? This is due to endorphins that our brain releases, which are natural, mood-enhancing hormones sometimes called the "happiness hormone." Although endorphins have a short-term effect, the better we treat ourselves through our nutritional habits, the better we feel all around.

Activity: Creatively build your own plate

Reflect

What does food have to do with the mind/body connection?
What are some ways that you can improve your habits in relationship to food?

> My nutritional habits are closely tied to my emotional and mental health.

Recreate!

To learn that balancing life means bringing harmony between our responsibilities and recreation

Write

What are your recreation and leisure activities?

1. _____
2. _____
3. _____
4. _____
5. _____

Understand

Our training and studies for the work we will do as adults should energize us, stimulate our growth and creativity, and give us great satisfaction as we accomplish our responsibilities and reach set goals. However, as exciting and fun as it should be preparing for our future and fulfilling tasks, it can bring a certain amount of stress to our lives.

Recreation is a way to take a break from the pressure-filled tasks that we accomplish in life. The word "recreate" so well expresses this important activity we do. Recreation should include new and fresh activities that stimulate our creativity, redirect our energies, and invigorate us for what is ahead. It is a way to relax and enjoy activities such as sports, spending time with friends, watching movies, being outdoors, playing games, riding bikes, listening to music, surfing the internet, etc.

This kind of entertainment often involves other people, so it also improves our social skills and communication. As we interact with others, we are better able to recognize and appreciate their interests and preferences. When we understand and apply the value of healthy recreation in relationship with those around us, we discover the importance of getting along with others and appreciating our differences. An additional benefit of recreation with others is that we will most likely end up discovering new activities to enjoy.

Although recreation time is important, it has to be balanced and should never interfere with our responsibilities. By regularly evaluating our priorities we will be able to keep an equilibrium in our life.

Tip

Talk to your parents or a teacher if you find it hard to balance your activities or if you experience stress. They may have tips for you to manage your time more efficiently.

Activity

Let's do something different!

1. Form groups of six and play during the time that is left in this lesson; it could be a board game, card game, making music, or a whole class activity (e.g., Heads Up 7up.) Let's be creative and spend time on some recreation!

2. Before the class ends, answer the following questions about the activity you played.
   - What activity was chosen by the group?
   - Why was that activity chosen?
   - What happened during the activity (positive or negative)?
   - What would you change about the activity? Why?

Apply

Create a life picture.

Take a piece of paper and write your name in the middle of a blank page. Decorate the page with activities that you think of as recreational (e.g., sports, video games, doing makeup, music, art, baking) and activities that you think of as responsibilities (e.g., homework, chores, babysitting). Look at the page when you are finished and determine how balanced your life is at this time.

Reflect

When you think of your recreational activities versus your responsibilities, what could you change to improve the balance in your life?

Do you have more fun doing recreational activities or responsible tasks? Why?

I can bring harmony in accomplishing my responsibilities and making time for recreation.

Get Active!

Goal To understand excercise and physical activities are important aspects of my health

Activity: With a partner, make a list of the benefits of exercise:

- _____
- _____
- _____
- _____
- _____
- _____
- _____

Write

Exercise provides many benefits! Being in motion positively affects us in diverse ways: physically, emotionally, socially, and mentally (or cognitively). That means our grades may improve the more active we are!

Define "Active": _____

Define "Sedentary":_____

1. Between a sedentary and active person, circle who you think is healthier. Why?
   _____

2. Make a list of sedentary activities you do in your day:
   _____ _____ _____ _____

   _____ _____ _____ _____

3. Make a list of physical activities you do in your day:
   _____ _____ _____ _____

   _____ _____ _____ _____

4. Look up the dictionary's definition of endorphins and write it here (or ask your teacher to provide the definition):
   _____
   _____

5. What stimulates the production of endorphins in your body?
   _____

6. What do endorphins do to you?
   _____

7. Why does exercise produce feelings of happiness?
   _____

Understand

Thanks to physical activity, blood flows better in the body, increasing the elimination of toxins through the lymphatic system (also a key way that infection-fighting white blood cells are transported throughout the body). The digestive system improves, and the increased frequency of breathing and heartbeats allows more oxygen to reach our organs. These and other positive impacts of exercise improve the growth and development of our body. Another great physical benefit of being active is that it helps regulate our metabolic system (i.e., how effectively our body processes food), and helps us maintain the best weight for our body type.

Moderate exercise also stimulates companionship, self-control, and discipline as it activates our brain power. This helps us produce a creative mindset as well as achieve better in school. As a result, our motivation to make wise and healthy decisions increases, which improves our behavior and ability to interact with others.

Regular exercise also helps to reduce stress, anxiety, and excess energy so we can maintain positive relationships with our family and friends.

Apply

Find a spot in the classroom where you can spread your arms without touching another student. Take 10 minutes to stretch different muscle groups, and be sure to breathe.

Notice your body and how it feels throughout these exercises.

Reflect

How did you feel during the activity?
What is one goal you can set related to your physical activity level?

I am committed to regular physical exercise because it is fundamental to me being healthy.

Health

Peer Pressure

To learn to stand for what I believe in and how to deal with peer pressure

 Read

Joe was a funny, well-liked 6th grader who had many friends. Joe didn't like to let others down or disappoint anyone. He did anything to make sure everyone always liked him. He rarely got in trouble because he wanted to please his teachers and parents as well.

One day, Joe was at the mall with a group of friends. They were at an expensive sporting goods store when his friend, Steve, tapped him on the shoulder and said that he was wearing a shirt from the store under his sweatshirt. He told Joe that it was easy and he'd done it before without being caught. Joe really wanted his favorite team's newest Nike shirt, but his parents wouldn't give him the money to buy it, saying he needed to find a way to earn it for himself. With Steve's pressure and assurance, Joe finally gave in and decided to go into the dressing room and put on the shirt he liked under his sweatshirt.

As he and his friends were leaving the store, the sensor started to beep. Mall security stopped the boys and searched them, quick to notice a tag showing from below Joe's sweatshirt. He was taken to the security office, where his parents were called, and they were fined triple the amount of the shirt. Joe's friend, Steve, was never caught. Joe felt ashamed, guilty, and sad, and wished he hadn't listened to his friend.

 Video
Watch the following.

flives.us/?i=96111

 Activity

- Get into groups of two and use the techniques from the video to role play.
- One student will play the role of Joe, and the other will be Steve.
- Come back as a big group and discuss what happened during the role play.

 Understand

There are three ways we can react: passive, assertive, and aggressive.

 Passive people avoid any type of confrontation at all cost, and almost always put the desires of others above their own. They prefer to react instead of taking initiative, use subtle manipulation, hold things in, and don't speak up. A passive person tends to believe that what they think isn't important; they often take the blame, feel powerless or guilty, and struggle to set strong boundaries.

 Assertive people tend to have a firm, open, honest, and clear delivery of a message. They use "I" statements, use the "broken record," believe their voice is important, set healthy boundaries, and are open and respectful of the opinions of others.

 Aggressive people tend to be more explosive when things don't go their way. They can be mean, short-fused, hostile, and rigid. They often use threats and ultimatums, have a need to be in control (but often feel out of control), and are often critical and put people down.

One way we can become more assertive, draw healthy boundaries, and better manage our life is to focus on others around us who struggle with peer pressure, just like we do. When we take a stand to help others and become a supportive voice for those who are easily influenced, we are better able to resist intimidation and to influence others around us in healthy ways.

 **Reflect**

How can you become a stronger, more influential leader in situations where your peers could get themselves into trouble or danger?

✔ I am a leader, I encourage others to be who they are by being assertive against negative pressure.

Coping with Stress

Goal   To recognize that stress is a normal aspect of life, and to learn how to manage it

Write a detailed list of activities that you do during the day (use page 42).
Which of these activities are important to you?

_____

Which of these activities are not important to you?

_____

Which of these activities are responsibilities?

_____

Which of these activities are time wasters?

_____

Comment (use page 42)
Life moves fast—people are often tired, nervous, irritable, and feel like they have no time.
When do you get stressed?
Why do you think it happens?
Do you think that if you learn to focus more on your priorities and spend less time on the things that distract you, you will experience less stress?

Understand
When we are stressed, the following physical reactions are triggered: our blood pressure rises, our breathing accelerates, our digestive system slows down, our heartbeat increases, our immune system declines, our muscles become tense, and we sleep less. It's not dangerous if it only happens now and then; however, when challenging circumstances extend and increase, our state of stress intensifies and it becomes a continuous condition as our entire being suffers. Our health, school performance, and even relationships with others may be affected. Too much stress for too long can cause disorders or disease.

We tend to believe that stress is a result of external circumstances. In fact, however, it is an internal process of how we react psychologically, emotionally, and physically to the challenging events in our environment. In order to confront them, our body mobilizes resources to protect us, which we define as stress—the automatic and natural response our body uses to deal with situations that threaten or challenge us. It either motivates us to flee situations as soon as possible, or to stay and confront them.

We actually need some stress in our lives because it helps us deal with danger, keeps us healthy, and enhances our life. While moving to a new home can cause positive stress, having a conflict with a friend or family member can cause negative amounts of stress. Learning to deal with stress and using it in our favor is a very important development in our life.

For example, as you leave 6th grade for life in middle school and high school, you will be confronted with increasingly diverse class schedules, and undoubtedly, more homework. How can you balance this type of stress in a healthy way?

 Activity: Quiz - How is your stress level?

Questions	Yes	Sometimes	No
Do you feel anxious?			
Do you react with rage/anger over little things?			
Do you often feel exhausted and tired?			
Do you have difficulty falling asleep?			
Do you ever wish you could run away from everything?			
Do you tend to be sick more often than your friends?			

 Apply: Tips for coping with and managing stress:

- **Change your environment:** Decorate, organize and clean your personal space (i.e., school desk/area, room at home, etc.) in a way that encourages you to be productive and positive. Keep clutter out of your life: choose a day once a week to de-clutter your personal space (i.e., throw out trash, put things back in place, etc.).
- **Organization:** Plan and prioritize tasks according to their importance and purpose. Take some time each day to write down your tasks and prioritize them.
- **Humor:** Learn how to relieve yourself from stress through "laughter therapy."
- **Recreation:** Learn how to release stress through recreational activities.

Reflect

Think about situations in your life that cause you stress.
Which situations cause you stress? Why?
What can you do to prevent and better cope with your daily stress?

 I can manage stress in a healthy manner and will find the tools to do so.

Living a Drug-Free Life

Goal

To develop a better understanding of why people use drugs and alcohol, and addressing these issues in my life

Video

Watch these two clips and make notes on your thoughts about the information given.

flives.us/?i=96141

flives.us/?i=96142

Comment

There is a great deal of information available about the many dangers of drugs and alcohol abuse. Some of the downsides include abuse, crime, addiction, and mental and physial illnesses. In this lesson, we will focus on the reasons why young people even start using drugs and alcohol.

Why do you think some children and teenagers start using drugs and alcohol? What can you do to maintain a drug-free life?

Activity

The class will be divided into two groups: one group will research the dangers and negative effects of drug and alcohol use. The other group will research alternatives to drug and alcohol use (i.e., what can be done to replace the use of these substances).

Both groups will create a Public Service Announcement (PSA) on their subject. Through the PSA, one group should inform others of the dangers and negative effects of drug and alcohol use. The other group will use their PSA to offer alternatives, suggestions, and tips on how to live a drug-free life.

This project may take 2-3 weeks and will be presented to the school via a video share. Make sure the video your group creates is interesting and memorable, with an impactful message.

Reflect

Explain in your own words the dangers and negative effects of using drugs and alcohol.

_____
_____
_____

What alternative would you choose instead of drugs and alcohol when an opportunity to participate in substance abuse presents itself?

_____
_____
_____

Complete the following:
I choose to live drug free because...

_____
_____
_____

It's up to me to be drug free and live my life to its fullest capacity.

NOTES

COMMUNITY

Discover how to interact with others, those who are like you or different from you, and how to contribute to society in a constructive manner.

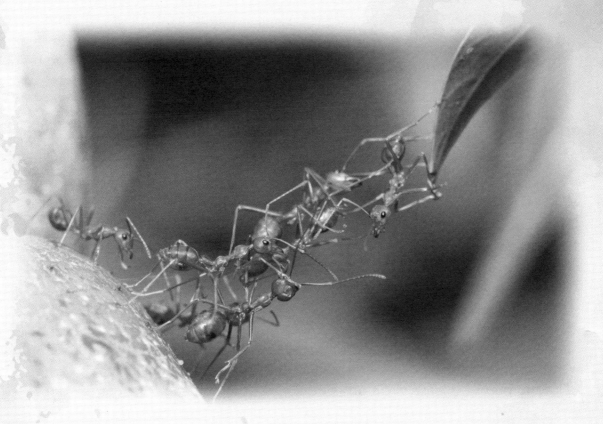

The people around you enhance your life and give you a sense of belonging. Together with others you can do and accomplish greater things, have more fun and become better at what you do. Serving others by sharing yourself through your skills, talents and being will enrich your life and give you great satisfaction. It also lays connections for hard times and challenging situations that life brings your way.

Empathy: What Is It?

Goal — To learn the definition of empathy and ways to put it to use

Video: Watch and learn

flives.us/?i=96161

This is the dictionary definition of empathy: identifying with the thoughts, feelings, or emotions of another person, especially in times of distress; it implies being tender-hearted.

It's like "walking in someone else's shoes."

Comment (Use page 58 to write your responses.)
1. Describe empathy using your own words. What does it mean to you?
2. Describe a situation when someone showed empathy toward you.
3. Describe a situation when you showed empathy toward someone else.

Activity
Sometimes it feels easier to show empathy toward some people than others. Students will vote from their seats by raising their hand to show empathy for the following people (please circle one or the other thumb as well in your textbook):

- a good friend
- someone who is less popular than you are
- someone who is very popular
- someone with a disability
- someone who has been mean to you in the past
- an adult
- a child
- someone your age
- a celebrity that experienced a tragedy
- someone who looks like you

- someone who looks different from you (gender, race, ethnicity, etc.)
- war victims
- people from another area, who's home was destroyed by a natural disaster

After the activity, students will have a whole group discussion about their thoughts.

 Understand

Empathy has to do with emotional intelligence (also called EQ, or Emotional Quotient), and therefore is a skill and habit that can be learned and used to truly understand where others are coming from, what they are feeling, and why (outrospection). It is a powerful tool to help us better communicate and interact with others, and to recognize what they are going through. Empathy increases the happiness level of others, as well as your own.

 Read: Words of Wisdom

The "Golden Rule" says to treat others as you would like to be treated. The flip side is: treat others how they would really want to be treated.

 **Reflect**

How can you show empathy at school and help prevent bullying? What does the expression, "See something, Say something" mean to you?
Are there other times you can show empathy at school? Please explain.

I use empathy as a tool to make my school a safer, friendlier place.

Personal Responsibility and Its Impact

To learn that I am responsible for my actions and how my actions are connected to my outcomes

 Read

As children, our responsibilities gradually increase as we grow older. As we learn to do things on our own, our confidence grows, as does our ability to manage various tasks. This is a natural process of life that happens under the guidance and supervision of adults and mentors who care for us. The helpful part is that they are already experienced in the life lessons we are learning.

Taking ownership for all our actions—positive as well as negative—is a very important skill we need to learn. Sometimes our actions can cause damage and destruction. And instead of blaming someone else or making excuses, it is critical we accept the consequences of our actions and take responsibility. When we do, we will realize that no one is perfect and that there is real value to learn from all of our actions. Once we learn to be fully responsible for our own actions, we will be able to see the effect and influence it has on others around us.

 Activity

Some people act irresponsibly and make excuses such as, "I don't have enough time," or "I forgot," or "I don't know how." Challenge yourself to write a schedule with tasks that you need to perform during the day. The daily calendar will show your responsibilities at home, at school, and play. Your teacher will give you a format for the calendar. A helpful way to remember your responsibilities is by writing a "to-do" list where you put the most important items at the top. You will experience satisfaction as you cross off tasks from your list.

After completing this schedule and your to-do list, place it somewhere you can see it so you can use it every day!

Understand

People around us recognize if we are reliable and whether or not we manage our daily tasks without constant monitoring. When we are dependable with our daily tasks, teachers, adults, and friends will begin to trust us with greater responsibilities. This will set the stage for when we will need to manage our lives on our own as mature and interdependent adults who are productive and responsible members of society.

To be a successful student and maintain an organized home life, there are routine tasks and jobs that need to happen (whether we like them or not). These activities can have a negative vibe because most of us don't find daily tasks pleasurable. As a result, we tend to have a negative attitude while completing them.

If we ignore these assignments and duties, they cause an effect like a snowball: as it rolls down the hill, it becomes bigger and bigger. Any responsibilities we have become more complex and difficult if we do not complete them in due time. One expression is, "If you don't have the time to do it right the first time, when will you find the time to do it over?"

Group work can help us successfully fulfill our personal responsibilities as others hold us accountable (i.e., help us stay on task). When work is distributed among a group, we learn about cooperation, autonomy, privilege, influence, and our ability to respond (responsibility). This is true teamwork in action.

Reflect

What does the word mature imply?
How can you maintain a positive attitude toward completing your tasks and assignments both at home and at school?
What are some things you would like to do, but lack experience in?
What leadership qualities do you possess?

When I faithfully complete my responsibilities, I am exposed to greater opportunities and privileges.

Lesson

19

The Power of My Words

Goal To understand that keeping my word makes me reliable and gives me authority (the power to impact my world)

Read

Josie, Tyler, and Sara are in the same Spanish class. On Wednesday, their teacher tells the students to choose groups to create a presentation together. The students will have only one day in class to work on the presentation, and will need to meet outside of class to complete it. Josie, Tyler, and Sara are friends, so they decide to work together. They have an easy time deciding on the topic of their presentation, and work well together during class. They agree to meet after school the next day in the library to finish their work; this will give them time to practice the presentation before they have to present it on Friday.

On Thursday, one of Sara's other friends asks her to go to the mall and hang out after school. Although Sara feels a little uncomfortable, she assures herself that Josie and Tyler won't care, and decides to hang out with her other friend instead of going to the library.

Josie and Tyler meet at the library after school on Thursday and work on the presentation as planned. When Sara doesn't show up, they are worried about her and annoyed, but decide she must be sick.

When Sara gets to Spanish class on Friday, both Josie and Tyler ask her why she didn't show up at the library. Sara says that her friend, Kayla, had asked her to hang out, so she did that instead. They are both upset with her, but they don't have time to talk about it because they only have 10 minutes to practice before presenting.

The next time the teacher allows them to choose their own groups, Sara asks Josie and Tyler to work with her, but they both say "no." Sara's feelings are hurt and she wonders if her friends don't want her to be in their group because she didn't show up the last time.

 Comment

Do you think Sara's choice had consequences? Please explain.
What does keeping your word have to do with your character?
Has anyone ever promised you something and then not done it? How did you feel?
Have you ever promised to do something and you didn't? How did you feel?
What benefits do you think keeping your word has?

 Understand

The formation of our character is of great importance because it tells others who we are. Our character is reflected in how we live: either if we act moved by positive values, or by negative influences and emotions. What we do and how we act when no one else is watching shows our true character—who we really are. A valuable characteristic is to keep our word and not change according to our convenience or the circumstances around us. If it happens that for some legitimate reason we cannot keep our word, we communicate as soon as possible with those we had an agreement with, ask forgiveness, and make it up to them (make amends).

We are reliable and trustworthy when what we think, say, and do are aligned; that's when we have authority. Think of a tree with deep roots and a leafy crown; it won't fall or change easily, as it stands firm. But someone who constantly changes their words is like a dead tree without roots and without fruit, easy to be knocked down, lacking strength and grit.

 Activity

What three words would you like others to use to describe your character?

_____ _____ _____

Make a poster to describe who your character shows that you are. Start out with I am….
Use the three words that you wrote above. Draw pictures, paint, make a work of art or write words or sentences.

 **Reflect**

Why is your character so important?
What do you need to do to improve your character?

My words have value.

Your Opinion and Mine

To be able to share my own opinions while respecting the opinions of others

 Comment

What is dialogue?

What is the purpose of dialogue?

What is your responsibility when engaging in a dialogue?

 Activity Part 1

Your teacher will post the following signs in a circle around the room: Strongly Agree, Agree, Disagree, Strongly Disagree. Your teacher will read a statement. Listen carefully! You will have 30 seconds to move to the area in the room that best reflects your opinion of the statement. When your teacher says to do so, students will discuss why they chose that spot. Remember to share your opinions respectfully, and listen to the opinions of others.

 Activity Part 2

All students will now vote on which topic they would like to discuss in more depth as a class. Once the vote has been taken, each group will have a turn to share their thoughts on the topic with the class, and will have the opportunity to respectfully respond to the other groups' opinions.

 Comment

When I communicate with other people, do I...

- interrupt when others are giving their opinion?
- listen to what others are saying, or am I focused on what I will be saying next?
- look others in the eye when they are talking?
- take turns to talk and to listen?
- like people to hear my opinion?
- feel impatient, irritated, or frustrated when others are giving their opinion?
- repeat what others said, to make sure I understood them correctly before I respond?
- see the value in others' opinions even though I might not agree with what is said?
- walk away remembering the other person's perspective?

 Understand

Dialogue is an art in itself and one of the most developed and complex ways that humans communicate. And while it is not the only one (we can express our opinions through

writing, music, dance, art, community activities, body language, etc.), it is the most-used manner of communicating on a daily basis. The notion of dialogue is directly related to the idea of living in a society that exists because of our ability to communicate with each other.

It is very important that we learn to express our ideas clearly and present them in a respectful way. It is equally important to listen and hear what other people have to say, and to value their opinions and perspectives. We need to learn that often times, others will not agree with our wishes, ideas, or opinions. This does not mean they are our enemies, but simply that they think differently. This often occurs with our parents, who because of their age and experiences, most likely have a different point of view from ours on many issues. One way to reach agreements and better understanding when we do hit a roadblock is to keep calm, ask them to express their thoughts, and if possible, share your thought. Another idea is to write down a list of options in the hopes of coming to a peaceful compromise.

Activity

Let's practice using dialogue to come to a consensus in a friendly way. The outcome will be a fun activity for the whole class!

Step 1: Form groups of four students.

Step 2: As a group, discuss a recreational activity that could be done at the end of the school year, such as a field trip, show, tournament, picnic, celebrity event, etc.

Everyone must come to a consensus and choose one activity.

Step 3: As you make your decision together, consider the cost, transportation, location, time needed, and other factors that would affect the likelihood of the event being approved by the school and parents.

Step 4: Choose one representative per group who will present the plan to the class.

Step 5: Peacefully choose one of the activities presented that the class would like to carry out at the end of the year.

Reflect

How can you clearly express your ideas while respecting the opinions of others? Make a list of words or phrases you can use.

I respectfully engage in dialogue and can peacefully come to a consensus.

I Make a Difference

To learn how to make a positive impact within my community

 Video: Watch and learn

 Comment

What does it mean to be a volunteer?
Have you ever volunteered to help with
some kind of activity? Please explain.
How did you feel after volunteering?

_____

_____

_____

flives.us/?i=96211

Understand

Volunteering and community service comes in
many forms. Everyone can find a way to make
an impact using their personal strengths, be
it through existing services provided by other
organizations, or personal initiative. Sharing
our time, thoughts, and talents can make a big
impact on people less fortunate than us, or those
facing serious challenges.

There are many ways we can be involved in
helping our community become a better place
to live. Someone who excels at building or
engineering can use this skill to help a local
organization build houses, wheelchair ramps,
or make repairs. Those who find themselves inclined to lead others can organize
a clothing, food, or toy drive to collect items needed by local members of the
community. Others may be interested in the arts, and can donate art to raise funds, or
perform for the local children's hospital or nursing home. Those who enjoy athletics
can help organize or volunteer with sports activities at a local youth center.

Groups are always looking for more hands to help. Activities like sharing our time with others by reading to children, visiting a nursing home or hospital can make a difference in the lives of others. We, ourselves, can start a volunteer group within our local community. Teens just like us are starting organizations and helping around the world. Each of us are inclined to lead in our unique way and each of us has the ability to join in and lend a helping hand to a cause.

Think about it: what talents or interests do you have that you can share with others to help make a positive impact in your community?

Activity

Form a group and brainstorm a community service project that your class can participate in within the local community. Here are some tips to help your group begin:

- Identify the needs inside your community.
- Identify the talents and interests of the group.
- Make a connection between the needs of the community and the talents and interests of your group.
- Within the local community, identify the groups that already exist and which needs they address.
- If no groups exist, brainstorm ways that your class can begin a group to help meet the unmet needs.
- As a group, make an action plan with which the whole class can participate in making a difference in your community.
- Create a presentation to share with the class.

The class will vote on one community service initiative to participate in together. If your group's project is not going to be the class project, help encourage friends and family to follow the mission that your group has started. Each one of us has the power to make a difference!

Reflect

Explain how you felt after participating in community service, and how your group impacted your community.

I use my strengths, talents, and interests to help those around me.

We Are Different, But Alike

Goal To appreciate the differences among us

Observe
Look at the pictures below of families eating a meal together.

Comment
Describe the similarities and differences you see in the images. Please explain.

Understand
Imagine if everyone dressed the same, ate the same food, spoke the same language and did the same things. How boring that would be! What makes our Earth so interesting is that it has a great variety of races with their own characteristics and customs. This offers us opportunities to learn about others and experience new things, enhancing our world through clothing, foods, traditions, and customs that are different than ours.

While we may look distinct, speak different languages, and have diverse traditions, no matter what we look like or where we come from, we all feel pain, happiness, sadness and love.

The mark of our humanity is how we treat each other. It is important to favor the disadvantaged, have compassion for the sick and feeble, love everyone as we love ourselves, welcome and honor the stranger and the different one among us, and help those in need. In a world where we see constant struggle and division between groups with contrasting opinions or cultures, we need to strive to lead by example. We can show our acceptance of others by recognizing and celebrating what makes us different, and find common aspects that unite us.

 Activity

Think of a unique tradition your family has and prepare a short presentation to share with the class. You can share pictures, objects, food, videos, etc., to help the class visualize and experience your tradition. The tradition can be small (Friday night game night and popcorn) or significant (a religious or cultural holiday).

Plan your presentation in the space at the right. Use extra sheets of paper if needed.

 **Reflect**

Which tradition presented by your classmates was the most interesting and different from those of your family?

Each of us is unique and valuable; I treat everyone with respect at all times.

23

Social Media and Me

Goal To recognize the great value of responsible use of social media

Read

Today it is common to be part of a social network. We use them to be informed on what is happening in the world, keep in touch with our friends, and stay on the cutting edge of affairs and commerce.

Write

Answer the following questions:
Describe what a social media network is.

_____

Are social media/networks necessary in your life? Why?

_____

Which social media/networks are you using the most? Why?

_____

How much time in a day do you dedicate to each social media/network you use?

_____

Are there negative aspects to social media networks? Please explain.

_____

_____

Understand

Social media networks are "virtual communities" where individuals and businesses communicate through internet services, platforms, sites, or phone applications. Their focus is to facilitate the construction of social contacts and relations between people who share interests, activities, or real-life connections.

Belonging to a social network helps us to build a contact group, which can be displayed as our "contact list." These connections can be personal friends, friends of friends, or even people we have never seen, nor know.

These wonderful services that connect us require our wisdom in their use. Here are some issues to consider:
1. With whom are we communicating: being virtual, we cannot be certain that the

person is who they say they are, or whether or not what they present to us is truthful.

2. What we share: once we post comments or photos on the internet, these take on a life of their own and remain there forever (even when deleted), and can be used against us.

3. How much time we spend communicating on social networks: if we wanted, we could be online 24 hours a day, which would seriously interfere with our vital tasks and relationships!

Activity

Working in a group, you will create a skit to demonstrate possible negative issues that can arise when using social media/networking, and ways to avoid this from happening. Write out a script, practice the skit, and present it to the class. Through this activity we want to demonstrate possible situations that can occur in the manner in which we use social media, and how we can prevent those situations from happening through responsible use.

Observe

Consider the two images. With a partner, discuss the impact of social media on relationships. Make a list of recommendations on how to use social media.

 ### Reflect

How can you be more careful with the information you give and receive while using the internet and social media networks?

How can you avoid being deceived on the internet?

> I use social media and networks responsibly, with care, and with balance.

NOTES

ENVIRONMENT

Discover the value of managing and protecting your home, planet Earth, with all its resources.

Wisely governing and sustaining Earth's resources is the key to ensuring a beautiful, productive and safe place to live for you, as well as for your children and all other living creatures.

Conserve and Protect

Goal   To understand my responsibilities and role in caring for natural resources

Observe

Go to the following website to learn why it is important to conserve and protect our environment. https://www.energystar.gov/index.cfm?c=kids.kids_index

Make notes here of at least 5 facts about energy challenges that stand out to you:

1. _____
2. _____
3. _____
4. _____
5. _____

Understand

One of our roles on Earth is that of caretakers. It is a full-time job that we acquire from the moment we are born until we leave this world, and it is a very important one.

Planet Earth provides us with many of the resources we need to live a long and abundant life. It is somewhat like a house, and just like our home, Earth needs

flives.us/?i=96231

continuous care, attention, organization, and replenishment. All this will only happen if we develop healthy living habits in dealing with the planet. Without these well-established habits, our Earth will degenerate and become disorganized, messy, used up, dangerous, and unlivable.

But even more, think about how you feel when you are in a quiet place in nature, versus how a busy street makes you feel. We are all responsible to do our part in carrying out the mission of taking care of our environment, be it the natural one as well as the constructed one. It is in our hands to ensure that future generations can enjoy all that nature has to offer. What can you do to make our world a better place?

 Activity

Imagine the impact on Earth if every person you know made a point to conserve energy and other natural resources! Work with a partner and check out the tips on the following website, and brainstorm some of your own. Your teacher will give you a location/activity that you will use as a theme for a project (poster, painting, clay model, woodwork, etc.) which you will prepare and present to encourage your school community to care for our Earth. Remember to be creative!

https://www.energystar.gov/index.cfm?c=kids.kids_index

Write: Record your ideas and write a rough draft of your project here:

_____
_____
_____
_____
_____

Use page 66 if you need more space.

Create: Record your rough design here:

Reflect

Complete the statement below:

I plan to _____ to do my part in attending to, caring for, and protecting my environment.

✓ **I take my role as caretaker seriously; I manage natural resources wisely.**

Our Animal Friends

To discover my role in protecting our animals

 Comment

What does "extinct" mean?

What does "endangered" mean?

What animals do you know of that have become extinct or are endangered?

What is an "ecosystem"?

 Understand

Imagine a world without animals. We use animals for food, clothing, and friendship, but why else do we need animals? Animals play a crucial role in maintaining a fine balance in our environment. For example, you might not like bees and other insects because of their stings and bites. But what if they disappeared completely? Bees and other insects are responsible for pollinating many of the plants we eat. These plants can produce fruits, vegetables, grains, seeds, and even the ingredients needed for developing important medicines.

Let's do some research to find out how we can help endangered animals, before it is too late.

 Activity

Research Project:

Step 1: Go online to discover which animals are currently endangered.

Step 2: Choose one endangered animal to research.

Step 3: Record the following information:

- Where does it live? _____
- What does it eat? _____
- Describe its habitat and any other interesting facts. _____
- Why is it endangered? _____
- What is threatening it? _____
- Why is it important to protect this animal? _____
- What does it do for our ecosystem? _____
- How can we help? _____

Step 4: Make a poster to display your findings; include pictures of the animal.

Step 5: Present your poster to the class.

 Reflect

Name one of the endangered animals you learned about from the presentations, and the steps you will take toward protecting this animal.

_____

_____

_____

I am motivated to stay informed on endangered species, and take steps toward their protection.

Endless Possibilities

To understand the importance of creativity when it comes to dealing with trash

Observe

We have the ability to give a different use to objects we utilize every day, and create other products from them.

What is this chair made of?

_____

What do the following 3 words mean to you? Give examples of each.

Reduce: _____

_____

Reuse: _____

_____

Recycle: _____

_____

flives.us/?i=96241

Video
Watch, learn, and be inspired

Understand

We all know that it is important to reprocess products and materials. Most of our communities have programs in place to recirculate used materials, but all those programs have little effect if we don´t cooperate. It is our responsibility to educate ourselves on the different guidelines and manners on how to recycle resources and follow through with them in our communities. Outside of the home, we can encourage others to create more opportunities for reprocessing materials. Does your local park have recycling bins? Does your school? Your favorite restaurant? We can always find

more ways and more places to recycle. But what about reducing and reusing? How can we do that?

Fortunately, more and more companies and individuals are creating alternative products and packaging that have less-destructive impacts on the environment. Being well informed on how the products we use affect us, as well as our environment, should motivate us to do our research and choose less-harmful products. Even replacing one everyday item, such as plastic grocery bags with a reusable cloth bag, can make a big difference.

What else can we do? Did you know that many products we use every day could be made from scratch using natural ingredients? Even shampoo! By being creative and making our own alternatives, we can save money, reduce waste, and use less chemicals that can harm both the environment and our health.

 Comment

What are some ways to reduce the amount of waste you produce each day?
What materials do you have at home that could be used for other purposes?

 Activity

Let's experiment!
Go online and find natural alternatives or "recipes" for the following products. Talk with the teacher about the possibility of making one of these products together.
1. A household cleaning product
2. Toothpaste or another personal hygiene product
3. Air freshener
4. Insect repellent

 **Reflect**

What can you do to help your family save money and care for the environment by reducing waste at home?

> I am creative; I find endless ways to reuse and recycle materials, and reduce waste.

NOTES

ECONOMICS

Discover how to become financially literate as well as understand the difference between wealth, value, and true success, and how to increase the resources that are available to you.

Your ability to create wealth with the resources available to you gives you the opportunity to uniquely share yourself with others and impact their well-being, which is fundamental to experiencing great satisfaction and happiness. That is how you design your legacy, or leave your fingerprint on humanity.

Wants Or Needs?

 Goal To learn to differentiate between my wants and needs so I spend and/or save my money wisely

Observe

Circle the pictures that show items you need (i.e., necessary for life), and put an "X" over items you want (i.e., not necessary, but you would like to have).

 Comment

Think about the things that you have at home. List a few items that you think are:

Needs: _____

Wants: _____

Understand

We tend to be a society that blends together our needs and wants. The constant advertisement of new and better products and our urge for "more" leaves us with full closets, rooms, and houses. It might feel good to be able to buy the latest model or new thing on the market. But does this really make us happy and fill our life with satisfaction? Have you ever stopped to think about this restless craving to constantly buy whatever is offered? How can all this excess in our life lead us to feeling stressed and overwhelmed?

As we grow older, we will become less dependent on our parents and how they spend money for us. As we learn how to earn money, it becomes critical that we understand how best to manage that hard-earned cash. An important step in the process is to be

able to tell the difference between what we need and what we want, so that we learn to spend and save our money wisely. A quick, impulsive purchase usually leads to regret, even though it might give us a moment of happiness.

Covering all of our expenses for the things we really need can be very challenging. For this reason, it is important to develop a habit of making lists before we go shopping. Our list can be composed of two parts: items we can't live without (necessities) and items we desire to have if there is enough money left over. Once the list is complete, we can move on to the next step and evaluate the items on our list using the questions below.

1. Is this item a need or a want?
2. If it is a want, is it something I think I will still want in a week, a month, a year? (Sometimes the true test is to wait a week or two to make the purchase, and then see if the desire is still there to buy it).
3. Is it something I already have or have enough of?
4. Is it worth spending my money on?

Activity

One way for us to help make our spending purposeful is to follow the rule of three: Spend, Save, Share. Find 3 containers in your house (jars from recycling, small boxes, etc.). Bring them to school where you will decorate them with "Save," "Spend," "Share." Afterward, take them home and place them where you will see them and be reminded to use them.

When you receive money for work or as a gift, divide it evenly into the three jars. When your save jar is full, take it to the bank to deposit it into a savings account. This money in the bank will work for you, earn interest, and grow even more. Keeping money in a spend jar at home, rather than in your wallet, will help you avoid impulse spending, and to better evaluate and plan out how you use it. You can use the money in the share jar when a group at school or in your community is collecting funds to help those in need, or to make your own purchases to donate to those in need.

Reflect

How will you use what you have learned in this lesson to spend your money more wisely and with purpose?

I share, spend and save my money wisely and with purpose.

What Is Priceless?

Goal — To understand that in life there are things that have no monetary value, but are valuable just the same

Write

Think of three things you would buy if you had an unlimited amount of money. Think of three things you would like to have, but that are not bought with money.

Things I would and could buy	Things I want that can't be bought with money

Comment

In life there are very expensive things and very valuable things. Describe in your own words the difference between something valuable and something expensive.

_____

_____

Do you have valuable things in your life? What are they?

_____

Understand

Some people mistakenly think that everything can be bought with money. In other words, they confuse expense with value. However, what is really valuable is derived from people and relationships, such as love, understanding, family, forgiveness, friendship, and much more.

What if there was a fire in your home? Losing your possessions would be extremely difficult, but the most valuable thing would be for your family (and pets) to get out safely and unharmed. Physical items can break and wear down over time; they can be stolen, or lost. True riches, however, stand the test of time. No one can take away the memory of a beautiful moment, or the smile of a loved one.

Being generous and compassionate will create priceless moments in our own lives and the lives of others, as well as valuable relationships that nurture us and help us grow.

70

Many people think that being generous is to donate money or give expensive gifts to others. But giving of ourselves through our time, company, service to others, words of encouragement, and love is often more valuable than any physical gift.

Activity

Working in a group you will discuss the following points and debate them. Before moving into groups, read over the presented statements and take note of your initial feelings.
Then, after the debate, you will evaluate if you still feel the same way.

Consider the following points:
- Wealth makes you happy.
- We need money.
- What is the purpose of money?
- When is a person prosperous?
- What are the signs of a successful person?
- Being rich means you have a lot of money.
- How do I avoid allowing money to control me?
- I control the money; money works for me.

Comment

Write your opinion of the debate.

_____

_____

Which statement held the most value for you?

_____

_____

Reflect

How much time do you invest in things that are truly valuable?
How can you invest more time and energy into things that are priceless in life?

I recognize and appreciate the truly valuable things and people in my life.

Lesson 29

Reach for the Sky

Goal

To learn to prioritize my activities and interests and become who I want to be

Observe

Look at the images below. What is important to you? What do you make a priority? Number the images from 1-8, #1 being the most important, and #8 the least important.

Comment

How did you choose the order of your priorities above?

Why is it important to prioritize your activities and interests?

Understand

Our priorities should be closely tied to our goals in life. For example, if we want to become an engineer, it is important to achieve good grades in school. Our top priorities should be to increase our knowledge and training. For many of us, that process starts at school. If our dream is to become a professional musician, what would be our priority? We prioritize time spent learning more about music, instruments, and time spent practicing. The good news is that you we still have plenty of time to explore what you want to do in the future to accomplish your destiny. When it comes to our future, however, it is never too early to start considering your priorities in order to set goals for both the short-term and long-term.

Apply: What are my goals?

Let's start thinking about our goals. Write one personal and specific goal for each of the following time periods:

1. Short-term: What do you want to accomplish by the end of this school year?
   _____

2. Medium-term: What do you hope to do after you graduate from high school?
   _____

3. Long-term: How do you see yourself in 20 years? What will you have accomplished?
   _____

Reflect

Evaluate your current top 3 priorities.
How can they help you achieve your goals?

Write: "Me in 20 years"

Write a paragraph explaining your goals and dreams for the long-term future. Explain how your priorities will help you reach your goals, and give examples of at least 3 specific steps that you can take in order to reach your goals.

_____
_____
_____
_____
_____
_____

I recognize that my goals can help me become the person I want to be.

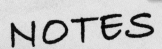

NOTES

NOTES

NOTES

NOTES

NOTES

NOTES

NOTES